PEOPLES OF THE
ANCIENT WORLD

Life of the
Ancient
Celts

Hazel Richardson

Crabtree Publishing Company
www.crabtreebooks.com

Crabtree Publishing Company
www.crabtreebooks.com

For Eben, Oliver, and Thomas

Coordinating editor: Ellen Rodger
Project editors: Carrie Gleason, Adrianna Morganelli
Editor: Rachel Eagen
Production coordinator: Rosie Gowsell
Production assistance: Samara Parent
Scanning technician: Arlene Arch-Wilson
Photo research: Allison Napier
Art director: Rob MacGregor

Project management:
International Book Productions, Inc.:
Barbara Hopkinson
J. David Ellis
Sheila Hall
Dietmar Kokemohr
Judy Phillips
Janice Zawerbny

Consultant: Lloyd Laing, Ph.D, Department of Archaeology, University of Nottingham

Photographs: ACE STOCK LIMITED/ Alamy: p. 29; Archivo Iconografico, S.A./ CORBIS: p. 27 (bottom); Art Archive/ Musée Alésia Alsie Sainte Reine France/ Dagli Orti: p. 26 (top); Art Archive/ Musée de la Civilisation Gallo-Romaine Lyons/ Dagli Orti: p. 23; Art Archive/ Musée des Beaux Arts La Rochelle/ Dagli Orti: p. 10; Ashmolean Museum, University of Oxford, UK/ Bridgeman Art Library: p. 9 (bottom), p. 21 (bottom); The British Museum/ Heritage Images: p. 9 (top); John Farmar/ Cordaiy Photo Library Ltd./ CORBIS: p. 4-5; Werner Forman/ Archives/ British Museum, London: p. 17; Werner Forman/ Art Resource, NY: p. 24 (top); Werner Forman/ CORBIS: p. 13 (middle), p. 18; Giraudon/ Art Resource, NY: p. 30; Giraudon/ Bridgeman Art Library: p. 11; Jason Hawkes/ CORBIS: p. 19 (bottom); Heritage Image Partnership: p. 26 (bottom), p. 27 (top); Dave G. Houser/ CORBIS: p. 22; Peter Hulme; Ecoscene/ CORBIS: p. 19 (top); Erich Lessing/ Art Resource, NY: p. 3, p. 8, p. 12, p. 13 (bottom), p. 21 (top), p. 24 (bottom), p. 25, p. 28; Private Collection/ Bridgeman Art Library: p. 31 (top); Michael St. Maur Sheil/ CORBIS: p. 31 (bottom); Nik Wheeler/ CORBIS: p. 29; Adam Woolfitt/ CORBIS: p. 7.

Illustrations: William Band: borders, pp. 4–5 (timeline), p. 6 (map of Europe), p. 7, pp. 14–15, pp. 16–17, p. 20, p. 23; Rob MacGregor: p. 10 (top)
Cover: A temple frieze, or wall decoration from Civitalva, Italy, depicting a Celtic warrior.
Contents: Dead bodies were buried in clay tubs in the ancient Celtic area of Hallstatt, Austria.
Title page: One of the entrances to a Celtic oppidum, or town.

Crabtree Publishing Company
www.crabtreebooks.com   1-800-387-7650

Cataloging-inPublication Data
Richardson, Hazel.
  Life of the ancient Celts / written by Hazel Richardson.
      p. cm. -- (Peoples of the ancient world)
  Includes index.
  ISBN-13: 978-0-7787-2045-4 (rlb)
  ISBN-10: 0-7787-2045-4 (rlb)
  ISBN-13: 978-0-7787-2075-1 (pbk)
  ISBN-10: 0-7787-2075-6 (pbk)
      1. Civilization, Celtic--Juvenile literature. I. Title. II. Series.
CB206.R53 2005
930'.04916--dc22   2005001102
                                                         LC

Published in the United States
PMB 16A
350 Fifth Ave.
Suite 3308
New York, NY
10118

Published in Canada
616 Welland Ave.
St. Catharines
Ontario, Canada
L2M 5V6

Published in the United Kingdom
73 Lime Walk
Headington
Oxford
0X3 7AD
United Kingdom

Published in Australia
386 Mt. Alexander Rd.
Ascot Vale (Melbourne)
V1C 3032

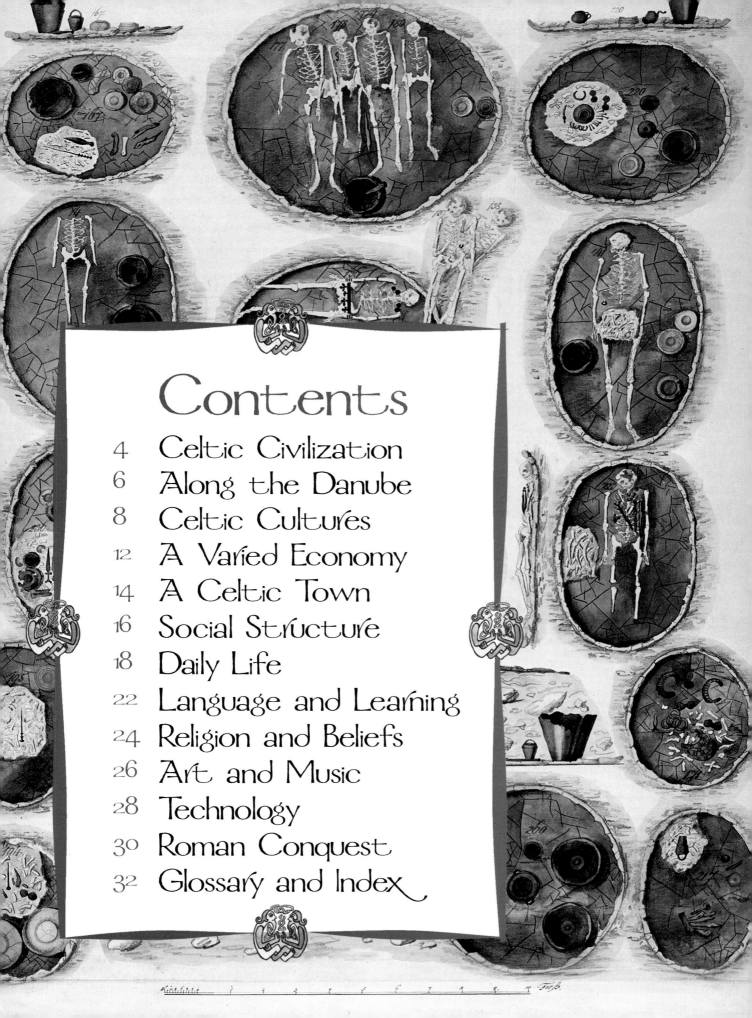

Contents

Celtic Civilization

The Celts were the dominant civilization in Europe from 600 B.C. to 50 B.C. From a few mining villages in what is now Austria, they expanded across central Europe and into the Iberian Peninsula in southwestern Europe. The Celts were fierce and fearless warriors, but they were also the most skilled and creative artists of their time.

Who Were the Celts?

There were at least fifteen different Celtic groups. Historians refer to them together as the Celts because they shared the same original language and way of life. Celts in different areas of Europe had their own **chieftains** or kings, and groups of Celts often fought each other. The Celts were eventually defeated by the **Romans**, but some of their **descendants** still live in western Europe.

Celtic Achievements

The ancient Celts built settlements on hilltops called hillforts, which were protected from attack by **ramparts**. The Celts were also fine metalworkers, and they traded with people from lands as far away as China. They were great warriors and inventors. Celtic inventions, such as chain mail, a type of armor, and iron horseshoes helped them in battle. Today, remains of Celtic communities are found across western and central Europe, from Ireland to the Czech Republic and Slovakia.

Hallstatt culture develops 750 B.C.

Bronze axe decoration from Hallstatt, Austria.

La Tène culture begins to develop around 475 B.C.

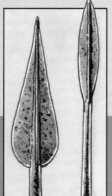

◄ *Iron spears and other weapons made by the Celts from the La Tène period were highly prized.*

Celts settle in Etruscan territory in present-day Italy in 400 B.C.

▼ *The Celts created decorative metalwork, such as this horse harness from Manerbio, Italy, around 100 B.C.*

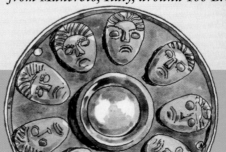

What is a "civilization"?

Most historians agree that a civilization is a group of people that shares common languages, some form of writing, advanced technology and science, and systems of government and religion.

▲ *Maiden castle, in present-day Dorset, England, was one of the Celts' largest hillforts. The Celts abandoned it more than 2,000 years ago, after an attack by Roman invaders.*

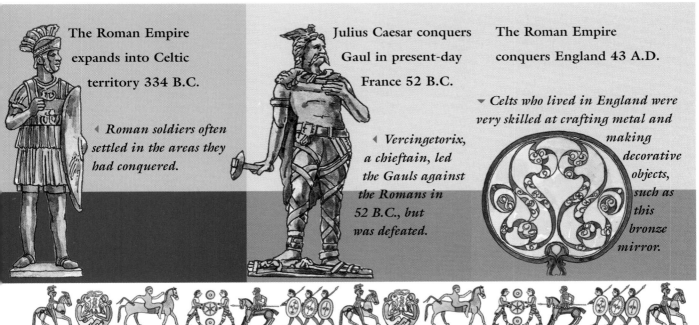

The Roman Empire expands into Celtic territory 334 B.C.

◄ *Roman soldiers often settled in the areas they had conquered.*

Julius Caesar conquers Gaul in present-day France 52 B.C.

◄ *Vercingetorix, a chieftain, led the Gauls against the Romans in 52 B.C., but was defeated.*

The Roman Empire conquers England 43 A.D.

▼ *Celts who lived in England were very skilled at crafting metal and making decorative objects, such as this bronze mirror.*

Along the Danube

The original homeland of the Celts was the Danube River Valley in what is now Austria. The Danube River Valley had plenty of fertile farmland and grasslands for grazing animals. A large mountain range called the Alps bordered their lands to the south, keeping the Celts safe from enemy attack.

◀ The Celts first moved from their homes in the northern Alps to search for more land. Other groups moved north into what is now Germany, south into present-day Italy, and west into the present-day British Isles.

Using the Danube

The Danube River, the second longest river in Europe, crossed westward from the Alps to the Black Sea. Each spring, waters from melting snow in the Alps caused the Danube to flood, depositing rich **silt** on the land in the river valleys. The silt made the soil excellent for farming, allowing the Celtic civilization to prosper and grow.

Alpine Life

The **lowlands** had large forests of oak and beech, and a variety of birds for hunting. The grasslands teemed with European bison and wild boars, which the Celts hunted for food. Boars were a catch prized by Celtic hunters because they were regarded as sacred animals. In the mountains, chamois, a horned antelope, was hunted for its hide, which was made into fine leather. Highland meadows, covered with grasses and poppies, lay between mountain peaks and were ideal food for grazing cattle and goats.

A Varied Climate

Some Celts gradually **migrated** from the Danube and the Alpine lowlands to the Po Valley in Italy. Others settled in central Europe in what is now Moravia, Slovakia, and Hungary, where the winters were cold. There, a lot of rain fell in the lowlands and valleys, and snow fell in the mountains. The summers were cool, but often sunny. Grains, such as oats, rye, and barley, grew well in this climate. The Celts moved south into what is now northern Spain, where there were mild winters and long, hot summers. Peas, beans, and wheat were major crop plants, and fruits, such as plums, were collected in the wild.

▲ *The boar was a favorite food of the Celts, and was the symbol of warlike strength.*

▼ *The Danube River Valley in present-day Austria was the Celts' original homeland.*

Celtic Cultures

In about 750 B.C., Celtic civilization developed in present-day Austria. There, Celts farmed the land and traded with the ancient Greeks **to the south. By 400 B.C., the Celtic population had grown so large that more land was needed to live on and farm. The Celts spread across Europe, splitting into different groups.**

Celtic Beginnings

Between 1300 B.C. and 800 B.C., a group of people **archaeologists** have called the Urnfield culture arose in central Europe. The culture was named for the container, called an urn, in which they buried their dead. The people of the Urnfield culture made weapons and tools from bronze and spoke an early form of the Celtic language. Historians believe that the Celts developed from the people of the Urnfield culture.

▸ *This iron mask and hands from Hallstatt, Austria, are covered with a sheet of bronze. The objects decorated a wooden urn that held the ashes of people who were cremated.*

◂ *The Celts were excellent metalworkers and made swords and other weapons out of iron. This iron dagger and scabbard, or case for the dagger's blade, are covered in a thin sheet of gold.*

The Early Celts

Many different groups of early Celts spread throughout the Alps. Most historians think the Hallstatt culture, which arose around 750 B.C., was the first Celtic culture. Another important early Celtic group was the La Tène culture, which arose around 475 B.C. in present-day Switzerland and France. From the La Tène culture, Celtic language and styles of artwork and metalwork emerged.

Raiders

Celtic groups in central Europe began to search for new farmland and trade opportunities, and raid nearby lands to steal gold, silver, and other treasures. From about 400 B.C. to 270 B.C., they began to settle in the areas they raided, such as present-day France, northern Spain and Italy, Germany, the **Balkans**, and **Bohemia**.

▲ *In battle, Celtic warriors protected their heads by wearing helmets made of iron and bronze.*

Battle Tactics

Celtic battle tactics depended on whom the Celts were fighting. If they were fighting against another Celtic clan, or group, only one man was sent into battle. The chieftains of both clans chose their best warrior to fight in a battle to the death. In battles against other peoples, the Celts lined up facing their enemy. They drank beer or mead, shouted insults at the enemy, sang war songs, and sounded war trumpets to scare the other army. Then, they charged on foot in a row, roaring and screaming. War chariots thundered along beside them. As the chariots reached the battle lines, warriors leaped off and entered the fight.

◀ *The Celts first used chariots as a means of transportation. They later used them to transport warriors into battle.*

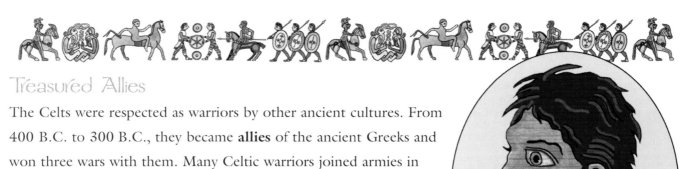

Treasured Allies

The Celts were respected as warriors by other ancient cultures. From 400 B.C. to 300 B.C., they became **allies** of the ancient Greeks and won three wars with them. Many Celtic warriors joined armies in Syria and Egypt as **mercenaries** and were paid well for their valuable fighting skills. In 259 B.C., Celtic warriors working for the Egyptian **pharaoh,** Ptolemy II, rebelled, and tried to establish a Celtic territory in Egypt. They were defeated by the rest of the Egyptian army, and left to starve to death on an island in the Nile River .

Rome is Conquered

The Celts' greatest success in battle was in 387 B.C. Led by a Celtic warrior named Brennus, Celtic raiders from northern Italy met the Roman army a few miles from Rome. The Celts defeated the mighty Roman army in one charge and invaded the city. After burning most of the city to the ground, the Celts **besieged** the Capitoline Hill, also known as the Capitol, the highest hill in Rome where the Roman government was located. The defenders stood firm for over six months and the Celts were unable to conquer the hill. The Celts left the city only after the Romans paid them an enormous amount of gold to leave and return to lands farther north. The Romans never forgot their defeat by the Celts, and there was an uneasy peace between the two civilizations for nearly 100 years.

▲ *Alexander the Great, the king of Macedonia, Greece, made an alliance with the Celts before he set out to conquer Asia in 335 B.C.*

◄ *When the Romans complained about the amount of treasure the Celts were being paid to leave Rome, Celtic leader Brennus is said to have thrown his sword onto the scale weighing the gold, making the Romans pay even more.*

Enemy Neighbors

Celtic groups that had settled new territories across Europe needed to defend the land against invasions by others. The Roman Empire began to expand into central and western Europe around 334 B.C. and conquer Celtic lands. Around 110 B.C., **Germanic groups** from northern Europe moved into Celtic territory. The many different Celtic groups were not unified under one leader, making them easier for invaders to conquer.

▼ Many Celtic sanctuaries, or holy places, contained human heads which the Celts offered to the gods. At Roquepertuse, France, the portico of a stone shrine displays human skulls.

Head Hunting

The Celts believed that a person's strength, courage, and wisdom came from their head. The greatest trophy for a Celtic warrior was an enemy's head. The Celts cut off the heads of opponents killed in battle, and tied them to their belts or to the bridles of their chariot horses. They also suspended the heads from the gateways and ramparts that surrounded their towns. The heads of their most powerful enemies were embalmed in cedar oil in chests, and kept in their homes. Possessing an enemy's head ensured good luck and success, and warded off evil from the fortress or home. Sometimes, Celts placed skulls in food storage pits to protect food from animals, insects, and rot.

11

A Varied Economy

The Celtic economy was based on agriculture, raising livestock, and trading. As the Celts expanded across Europe around 400 B.C., they took control of mines and other resources.

Agriculture

Most Celtic families raised their own animals, such as cows and pigs, for meat and skins. Families also grew vegetables, wheat, barley, and oats. The Celts used iron plowshares to work the fields. Plowshares are metal blades that cut loose the top layer of soil that is being cultivated, or prepared, for farming. The use of the iron plowshare made it easier to plow the heavy clay soil.

Mining

Salt was one of the Celts' most important trade goods. Salt was valuable in ancient times because it was used to preserve meat and fish, or stop them from rotting. One of Europe's largest salt mines was in the early Celtic settlement of Hallstatt, in Austria. The Celts dug deep shafts, or narrow passages, into the mountains to reach the salt. Tin was another valuable mining product of ancient Europe. Tin was needed to make a metal **alloy** called bronze, from which tools and other objects were crafted.

Desirable Goods

The Celts produced many goods that other ancient cultures wanted. The Celts traded salted fish, wool and woolen cloth, leather goods, helmets, and armor. Celtic ironwork was the finest in the ancient world, and their weapons and tools were prized trade items. With the wealth they acquired through trade, the Celts bought many precious goods, including wine and bronze wine goblets from Greece, silk from China, and glass beads from Egypt.

▲ *Miners in the Hallstatt salt mines used simple tools, such as pick axes and wooden shovels, to dig out the valuable salt.*

Trade Routes

The Celts controlled many important trade routes in Europe. The Danube River was the major trade route for goods between Celtic lands and the Mediterranean. A group of Celts in Bohemia controlled the Amber Road, the main trade route for amber. Amber is a semi-precious stone formed from tree resin, or sap, that dried out millions of years ago. Amber was plentiful in the area known today as the Balkans. The Celts also used the Amber Road to trade other goods with the ancient Greeks, who were one of the Celts' most important trading partners. Celtic traders from the Alps traveled through difficult mountain passes to reach the Greek trading city of Massalia, which is today the French city of Marseilles.

Celtic Currency

When the Celts began to trade with other civilizations, they used iron bars and sword-shaped iron pieces as money. The first Celtic coins were made in 320 B.C. These were replicas of gold Greek coins and often depicted images of horses, the Celts' favorite animal in art, and wild boars. The Celts made coins from copper, silver, gold, and tin.

▶ *This Celtic coin depicts a horse with a human head leaping over a boar.*

▼ *Wealthy Celtic women were buried with jewelry, such as this amber necklace that was found in a grave in Austria.*

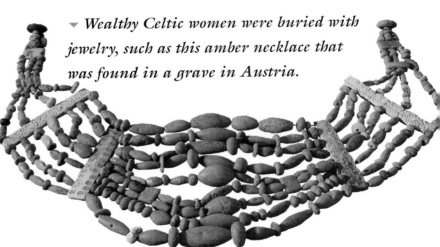

▲ *Archaeologists found a miner's wooden pouch and leather and fur cap at the salt mine in Hallstatt, Austria.*

A Celtic Town

Some Celtic towns evolved from fortified **settlements called hillforts. Others were built near rivers, in valleys or on plains. These towns, called oppida by the Romans, were built on major trade routes. Oppida were fortified to keep their inhabitants and goods safe from enemy attacks.**

1. Houses built by Celts who lived in Europe were usually rectangular, but in England and Ireland, some houses were round. They were constructed of timber and had **thatched** roofs of straw and reeds.

2. Craftsmen, such as blacksmiths, who made tools and weapons from iron, copper, and bronze, lived and worked inside the town.

3. The wall surrounding a Celtic town was about sixteen feet (five meters) high. To make a wall, planks of wood were nailed together with iron nails. Stones and earth were heaped up on both sides of the wooden wall to make a thick defensive barrier. Some towns were protected by two or more walls.

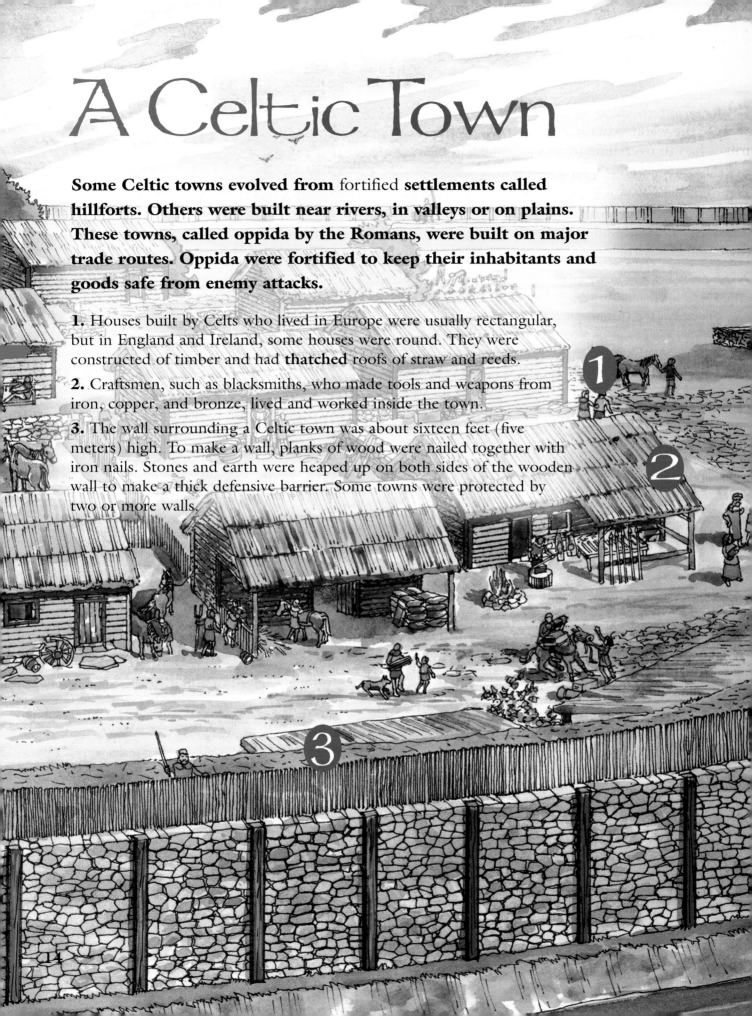

14

4. Towns were often built alongside streams or rivers because the water was a natural barrier that enemy armies had to overcome to conquer the town.

5. Most towns had at least two entrances. These were narrow, which prevented a large group of enemy warriors from rushing the gates together. From the ramparts, defenders could easily attack anyone trying to storm the gates.

6. Sanctuaries served as places for the town's inhabitants to worship the Celtic gods and to make **sacrifices** to them. The sacrifices, which were people and animals, such as horses, were thrown into pits inside the sanctuaries.

15

Social Structure

Celtic communities were made up of clans. Clans were extended family groups that lived together on and farmed a small plot of land. The head of the clan was a king or queen, or an elected chieftain.

Kings, Queens, and Chieftains

There were many rulers at any one time in Celtic lands, as each clan had its own king or queen. To be respected, rulers had to be physically fit, show their wealth, and provide their followers with feasts. Their close relatives made up a class of wealthy **nobles**. Celtic kings and queens always belonged to the family of the clan's last ruler. In clans ruled by chieftains, the leaders were elected because of their skill in battle and leadership.

Druids

Druids were ancient Celtic priests, teachers, and doctors, and were considered the most important people in the community. At least one druid lived in each community. Versed in Celtic histories and knowledge, druids performed religious ceremonies and offered sacrifices to Celtic gods. They also created laws that described how to behave, and acted as judges when someone was accused of a crime.

Celtic Social Structure

Kings and Queens

Druids, Chieftains, and Nobles

Artisans and Bards

Farmers, Workers, and Warriors

Warriors

Working men in Celtic communities were expected to go to war when their king or queen commanded it. Celtic warriors stripped naked and often painted their bodies with woad, a blue dye, to frighten their enemies. They carried wooden or wicker shields, sometimes covered with leather. Their weapons consisted of swords and spears, and they fired stones from a leather sling.

Skilled Artisans

Artisans were people who mastered a craft. Blacksmiths, engravers, and glassmakers were paid to make jewelry, weapons, and tools. Learning a skill was a common way for farmers to become wealthier. The children of artisans usually trained to do the same job as their parents.

Wandering Bards

Musicians and poets, known as bards, were highly respected, as their job was to learn the Celtic histories, stories, and legends and recite them as songs or poetry in each community. Bards also carried news between clans.

A Farming Folk

Most Celts were farmers and animal herders who lived on small **homesteads**. Their clan ruler controlled the land they farmed. Farmers paid their king or queen a part of their harvest each year in return for the use of the land and for his or her protection.

▲ *Artisans, such as bronze workers, used spatulas made of bone to shape beeswax models of pieces to be cast in bronze.*

Celtic Women

Some Celtic women were rulers, and many others were druids, bards, or artisans. Women owned property, chose their husbands, and could divorce and remarry if they wished. Some women trained as warriors, although most looked after the children, cooked food, wove cloth, and made pottery for the home.

Daily Life

Most clans lived together in small farming communities. Every house was shared by three generations of a family, including children, their parents, their unmarried aunts and uncles, and their grandparents.

The Homestead

Most Celtic families lived in a farming homestead surrounded by an earth wall or a fence of sharpened logs for defense, called a palisade. The homestead consisted of a main house, a dairy, a smithy, a granary, and sheds for the animals. Across Europe, rectangular houses were common, and some houses in Britain and Ireland were round. Walls were made from stone, planks of wood, or from a wooden frame covered with plaster made of mud and straw. Celtic houses had a single room inside. A fire pit made of flat stones was situated in the center of the room, and a hole in the thatched roof allowed the smoke to escape. Inside the home, the family sat and slept on blankets made of animal skins or woven wool.

▸ *Celts in Britain and Ireland built large, circular houses similar to these reconstructions. Each house was almost 50 feet (15 meters) in diameter.*

▲ *Broch were round towers with hollow walls built from stone. Many broch have been found in Scotland. Celtic kings built the towers to protect their settlements from sea raiders.*

Hillforts

Many Celtic communities built stone or wooden forts surrounded by ditches and high walls on a hill to shelter in during attacks. These were called hillforts. During attacks, the local ruler and his or her family sheltered in a large, central building, while the rest of the community stayed in wooden huts built around it. Warriors defended the fort from behind the earth and stone walls.

◀ *Hillforts, such as Old Sarum in Salisbury, England, overlooked the land and protected the Celts from attack.*

Celtic Menus

The Celts' most common meal was porridge made from oats. They also ate stews made with meat and vegetables, such as turnips and beans, accompanied by small loaves of bread. Bread was made from barley, rye, or wheat flour. The most popular meats were boar, pork, beef, deer, and bear. To wash the food down, Celts drank beer that was brewed by soaking grains, such as wheat or barley, in water. When the grains started to sprout, they were drained of the water and roasted over a fire. Then, they were boiled in water and **yeast** was added. The brew was left for several weeks while the yeast acted on it. It was then strained to remove the grains. Mead, another common drink, was made in the same way, but honey was added to the water to make it sweeter-tasting than beer.

Every Last Bit

The Celts did not waste any part of an animal that they killed. They made hundreds of different items from animal bones, such as needles, shovels, tool handles, and musical instruments, such as flutes. Leather goods, such as shoes and belts, were made from animal skins, and drinking vessels were made from animal horns.

Feasts and Fighting

Kings and queens held feasts in their homes or outdoors to keep clan members loyal to them. Everyone in the community was invited to attend and eat as much as they wanted. Roasted meats and loaves of bread were served with large amounts of beer and mead. During the feasts, bards told tales and songs were sung. Warriors carried out pretend battles to show off their fighting skills.

▲ *Celtic kings held great feasts with music, story telling, and mock battles.*

▼ *The Celts made bread from wheat flour.*

Celtic Children

From an early age, children were expected to help their parents in the home. Girls were taught how to spin wool and weave cloth, make butter and cheese, cook, and make simple pottery. Boys helped in the fields with the animals, and other farm work. Boys, and girls, if they wished, were taught how to fight with a sword and spear.

Celtic Dress

Celtic women wore floor-length dresses made of woven cloth, and wealthy women wore linen and silk dresses. Belts were made of leather or bronze chains. Men wore shirts and knee-length **tunics** made of linen cloth. Wool was woven into cloth to make warm trousers for the men, long skirts for the women, and cloaks that were fastened with decorative brooches. Both men and women wore leather shoes or sandals.

Celtic Beauty

Celtic women styled their hair with combs made from bone. Hair was worn straight, curled, or in braids, and was decorated with combs and ornaments. Women used oils and sweet herbs as perfume. Celtic men braided or spiked their hair, and often bleached it with **lime** water. Archaeologists have found many mirrors and razors, which they believe were used by nobles.

▲ *The Celts spun wool with weaving combs made from animal bones and antlers.*

▲ *(top) The Celts wore brooches, finger and ankle rings, and necklaces made of gold.*

Language and Learnir

The Celts did not write down their history. Instead, they passed on information through stories. Clan members, usually druids, memorized the stories and re-told them to others.

Spoken Languages

Celtic groups in different areas of Europe spoke slightly different forms of the Celtic language. The most common language spoken by the Celts who lived in present-day France was Gaulish. The Celts in Britain spoke British, which was nothing like modern English. The Celts in Ireland spoke a language known as Gaelic. Beginning around 100 B.C., Celts began to use Latin instead of their own language as the Romans slowly conquered their lands. By 400 A.D., most of the Celtic languages were no longer used. In some areas, the languages survived, such as Brittany in France, Wales and Scotland in Britain, and in Ireland.

Writing

At least 500 years after the Celts were introduced to the Greek alphabet, they developed their own alphabet for writing called the Ogham script. The Ogham alphabet was made up of 25 letters, with consonants written as a series of vertical or horizontal lines. Vowels were written as dots. Archaeologists have found many gravestones and stones used to mark boundaries engraved with Ogham script in Britain and Ireland.

▶ *According to Irish legend, Ogham script was invented by the god, Ogma.*

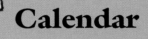

Druid Schools

Each Celtic community had one or more druid who educated the children of nobles. Between the ages of seven and fourteen, girls and boys were taught Celtic histories and religious beliefs by listening to the druids. The druids did not believe in writing down their knowledge and students had to memorize all their teachings. Lessons were often sung in songs and students had to sing the songs until they were known by heart. Some children were also taught to read and write Greek script for everyday use.

▶ *Druids, ancient Celtic priests and priestesses, taught the children of nobles, who had to memorize their teachings.*

▲ *An ancient Celtic calendar, called the Coligny Calendar, still exists. It was engraved on a large, bronze plate and was written in ancient Greek script.*

Calendar

Pieces of a large bronze tablet were discovered in the town of Coligny in southern France in 1897. Archaeologists believe they are the remains of a Celtic calendar created by druids around 100 A.D. If the calendar is authentic, it shows that the Celts had twelve months, each consisting of 29 or 30 days. This made the year 354 days long. Every third year, an extra month was added to keep pace with the movement of the Earth around the sun.

Religion and Beliefs

The Celts believed that different gods controlled all aspects of life on Earth. Many gods and goddesses were thought to live in and near water. Celts made sacrifices to the deities **to gain their help and approval.**

Sanctuaries and Sacrifices

The Celts worshiped their gods in forests by springs, rivers, and lakes, or at shrines and in sanctuaries. Sanctuaries were rectangular or circular buildings constructed in woodlands by water, or in the cities. Artisans worked at the sanctuaries in the cities, making gold and silver coins and decorated swords for visitors to toss into the sanctuary. Ditches and palisades surrounded the sanctuaries as a defense against raiders. Inside the sanctuaries, live animals, most often horses, were thrown into pits as offerings to the gods. People were sometimes sacrificed at the sanctuaries as well.

Spiritual Leaders

Druids were the spiritual leaders of the Celtic community. Druids not only memorized Celtic stories, histories, laws, and religious beliefs, they also predicted the future by observing signs, called omens, in nature. This practice is called divination.

▲ *Votives, or presents, were placed in the graves of dead Celts as offerings to the gods of the Otherworld.*

◄ *Many votives, such as this man in a boat, were carved from wood. The Celts believed that trees, especially oak trees, were sacred bridges between the people on Earth and the gods in the sky.*

The Otherworld

The Celts believed that after death, a person's spirit went to the Otherworld, where spirits lived before they were born and after they died. In the Otherworld, warriors attended feasts at which **cauldrons** of beer and mead never emptied and animals were made whole again after being eaten. Some Celts believed that people could visit the Otherworld while still alive by finding secret, hidden passages in nature.

Burial Mounds

Kings, chieftains, and nobles were buried in enormous mounds of earth. Each mound had one or more wooden burial chambers inside it. Items that the Celts believed the dead person needed in the Otherworld were laid around the body. Warriors' burial chambers were filled with spears, swords, and shields. The graves of kings and queens contained chariots, silk cloth, and amber and glass beads. Working people were **cremated** or buried in simple graves with small offerings, such as brooches.

Celebrating the Seasons

The Celts celebrated each season with a religious festival of feasting, games, and sacrifices to the gods. The start of spring was celebrated on February 1, at the Imbolc feast, which was a **pastoral** festival. The Celts held the festival of Beltane on May 1, to celebrate summer. Druids herded cattle between two bonfires as a **ritual** to keep them healthy, and houses were decorated with greenery to welcome fertility to farms. The Feast of Lugnasad celebrated fall. The festival began on August 1, and lasted for a month. Samain, held on October 31, celebrated the start of winter. Samain was the most important festival because it was believed that the powers of the Otherworld were let loose on Earth. Human and animal sacrifices were made to please the gods of the Otherworld.

◀ *A bronze krater, or vessel for blending wine, was found inside the Vix burial mound near Mont Lassois, France. The Vix mound covered the grave of a Celtic woman, known as the Princess of Vix.*

Art and Music

The Celts were fond of decoration, and made gold, silver, and bronze ornaments for themselves and their horses. They were also known throughout the ancient world for their music, stories, and intricate artwork.

Animal Gods

Most of the gods worshiped by the early Celts were animal spirits. The Celts made metal and wooden figurines of horses, boars, and bulls that were offered to the gods as votives. After trade with Greece and other nations increased, the Celts began to worship statues of gods and goddesses that had human bodies, as did the Greeks and the Romans. Most of these Celtic gods still had some animal features, such as the god Cernunnos, who was always depicted with horns.

Myths and Legends

The Celts told stories of heroes and adventure. The stories were written down long after the Celtic culture declined, but they reveal the types of stories druids and bards told 2,000 years ago. One of the most famous stories is that of the Celtic hero, Cú Chulainn, from Ireland. In it, the queen of Ireland sends her men to capture a bull from Cú Chulainn's clan. Cú Chulainn single-handedly defends his people and protects the bull from the queen's men.

◀ *Cernunnos was the god of life, animals, and wealth. His name means "the horned one."*

▲ *The goddess Epona was the protector of horses and riders. She was often shown as a woman sitting sideways on a mare.*

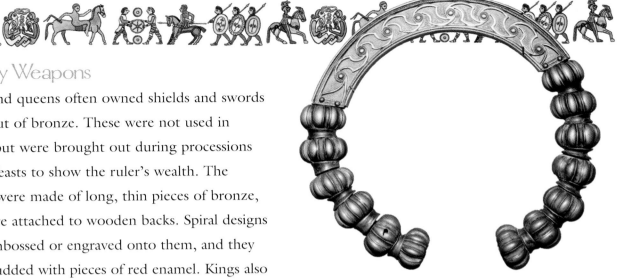

Display Weapons

Kings and queens often owned shields and swords made out of bronze. These were not used in battle, but were brought out during processions and at feasts to show the ruler's wealth. The shields were made of long, thin pieces of bronze, and were attached to wooden backs. Spiral designs were embossed or engraved onto them, and they were studded with pieces of red enamel. Kings also had bronze helmets made for display with plumes of horsehair attached to the top.

▼ *The Celts invented enameling as a form of decoration for jewelry, weapons, and bowls. Melted colored glass was poured onto bronze, silver, or iron objects, which cooled into a hard shiny pattern, like the design on this shield.*

Artwork Styles

Celtic designs were some of the most unique and beautiful in the ancient world. Early Celtic art had repeating patterns of triangles, lines, and rectangles, or maze-like patterns running along an item. By 400 B.C., decoration had become more detailed and complex. Fine spirals, leaf shapes, and images of birds, animals, and trees were engraved on metal and wood. Faces of people and animals were often hidden in the patterns and could only be seen when looking at the artwork very closely.

Music

The Celts played music in their homes for entertainment in the evenings. Most people made flutes and whistles from bone or wood. Bards told their stories or poems accompanied by drumbeats or simple music played on a flute or a stringed harp. Chieftains owned highly decorated wooden and bronze horns that they used to call warriors to battle, to signal during hunts, and to play at feasts. Many horns were decorated with carvings of animals, such as wolves.

▲ *Neck and armbands, called torcs, were a sign of wealth and status in Celtic society.*

Technology

The Celts were the most advanced metalworkers in the ancient world. They used their skills to make tools for farming and mining, as well as weapons and armor that helped them succeed in battle.

Iron Smelting

Europe had huge amounts of iron ore in ancient times. To extract the metal from the ore, the Celts **smelted** the rock using a furnace. The furnace was a tall, cylinder-shaped chimney built from long sticks covered with clay. **Bellows** blew air into the furnace through small holes in the furnace walls, making the fire inside very hot. **Charcoal** was set on fire and poured into the furnace from the top. Then, iron ore and more charcoal were added to the furnace for over an hour or more after which raw iron had formed on the bottom of the furnace floor.

▲ *A bronze hub, or center part of a wheel, was found inside the Vix burial mound in France.*

Chariots and Chain Mail

War chariots were one of the Celts' most effective pieces of battle equipment. They were used to transport Celtic warriors into battle. Pulled by two horses, the chariot cart was made of woven wicker, which made it light and quick. The cart was very low at the back and front so that warriors could climb in and out of it easily. The Celts invented iron tires for the wheels, which helped the chariot to move quickly. The Celts also made shoes for their horses from iron. Horseshoes reduced the risk of horses injuring their hooves as they galloped over rocky ground. Chain mail was another Celtic invention. Chain mail was a type of armor, usually a vest, made up of thousands of connecting metal rings.

Coracles, Canoes, and Ships

The Celts used three types of boats for traveling on rivers and across lakes: coracles, canoes, and ships. Coracles, or curraghs, were egg-shaped boats designed for one person. Consisting of a lightweight frame covered with leather, coracles were also used as sleds to haul goods in winter. Heavy canoes were hollowed out of tree trunks and used to paddle across waterways. Trading ships were even larger. Long and narrow, and equipped with leather sails, they could hold up to eighteen men, who would row when the wind was not blowing in the direction they wanted to sail.

Celtic Medicine

The Celts were skilled herbalists, using plants to treat and cure illnesses. Seaweeds were used to treat headaches, garlic was given to people with bladder problems, and the herb tansy was brewed into a tea for stomach problems. Mistletoe, a plant with white berries that grows high up on trees, was used to cure various ailments, such as swelling.

▲ The Celts believed that a sprig of mistletoe, especially if found growing on the sacred oak tree, had the power to heal humans of many illnesses.

◄ The Celts used coracles to fish and for transportation. Their light weight made them easy to carry.

Roman Conquest

The end of Celtic dominance in Europe arrived when Julius Caesar, a Roman general, conquered most of their lands, beginning around 58 B.C. Celtic ruins can be seen in many European countries today. Their fortresses, burial mounds, and boundary stones dot the countryside, and new excavations are made every year.

The Conquest of Gaul

When the Romans met the Celts living in France, they called them the Gauls. Julius Caesar battled a Celtic group called the Helvetii to keep them from migrating westwards into France. After defeating the Celts, Caesar decided to conquer the rest of Gaul so that Rome could control the major trade routes for amber and tin. In 52 B.C., led by a Celtic chieftain named Vercingetorix, the Celts made a final stand against the Romans at a hillfort in France. The Romans surrounded the fortress, and the people inside slowly starved to death.

England

In 43 A.D., Claudius, the Roman emperor, ordered the invasion of England. His army quickly conquered the Celtic groups of southeast England. Some Celts welcomed Roman innovations and the building of new towns and roads after the conquest. Many druids fled into present-day Wales to avoid being captured and killed by the Romans. Most Celts in England took on the Roman way of life, languages, and religion. In other areas, such as Ireland, Celtic laws, languages, and oral histories continued to survive.

▶ *After the Celts were defeated at their hillfort, Alesia, in France, Vercingetorix surrendered to Caesar's army. He was then taken to Rome, where he was executed.*

Scotland and Ireland

The Romans moved steadily northward through Europe, conquering Celtic groups as they went. The Romans never managed to conquer the Celts in the highlands of Scotland or in Ireland. The Celtic culture in Ireland remained intact well into the 400s A.D. when Christianity was introduced to the Celts. Christianity follows the teachings of Jesus Christ, believed to be the son of God. Many Celts **converted** to Christianity, but adapted some of their way of life into their new religious beliefs.

Celtic Crosses

Hundreds of stone crosses were raised in Ireland and Scotland by Celtic Christians. The crosses combined a circle, the Celtic symbol for the moon, and the Christian cross. The designs on the crosses, such as spirals, keys, and knot work, were copied from those used in Celtic metalwork.

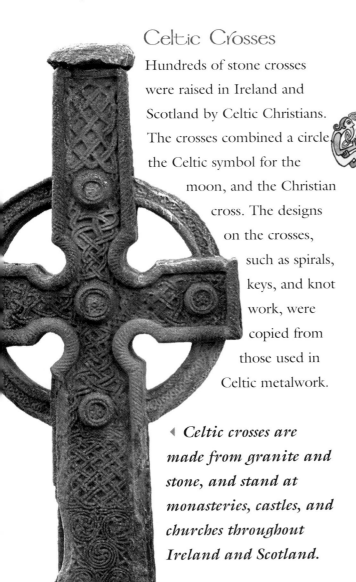

◀ *Celtic crosses are made from granite and stone, and stand at monasteries, castles, and churches throughout Ireland and Scotland.*

The Bravest Queen

Boudica was the Queen of the Iceni, a Celtic tribe from England. When her husband, King Prasutagus, died in 60 A.D., the Romans seized his lands. When Boudica demanded the lands be returned to her, the Romans whipped her. The queen then gathered her warriors, and set out on a battle of revenge. Her army burned down the new Roman cities in England, including London. Roman backup troops soon arrived, and most of Boudica's warriors were killed. Rather than be captured, Boudica killed herself with poison.

▲ *Boudica ordered that all Celts who had supported the Romans be killed.*

Glossary

allies People or countries that have partnerships or friendships with each other

alloy A mixture of two or more metals

ancient Greeks People who lived in the present-day country of Greece over 2,000 years ago

archaeologist A person who studies the past by looking at buildings and artifacts

Balkans A peninsula of southeast Europe

bellows An instrument used to pump air

besiege To surround with an army in order to capture

Bohemia A region in present-day Czech Republic

cauldron A large vessel or pot used for boiling

charcoal A material made of carbon produced by heating wood or plant and animal material, and used as fuel

chieftain The leader of a group of people or clan

convert To change from one religion or belief to another

cremate To burn a body after death

deity A god or goddess

descend Relating to a certain family or group

excavate To uncover by digging

fertile Able to produce abundant crops, vegetation, or offspring

fortify To make strong or defend, as against attack

Germanic groups Celtic tribes of German origin

homestead A farmhouse surrounded by land and other buildings

lime A white chemical, also called calcium oxide, which is used in making mortar and cement

lowland An area of low, flat land

mead An alcoholic drink made from honey

mercenaries Soldiers hired for money to work in the armies of other countries

migrate To move from one region into another

nobles People who have a high position in society

pastoral Relating to the country or country life

pharaoh A king, especially from ancient Egypt

rampart A wall or bank of earth raised around a structure for protection against attack

ritual A religious ceremony

Romans A group of people from what is now present-day Italy

sacrifice An offering to a god or a goddess

shrine A place that is devoted to a god or gods to honor them

silt Soil that is carried by water that settles on the bottom of lakes or rivers

smelt The process of removing metals from rock by using extreme heat

thatched Straw or grass woven to make a roof

tunic A long, loose piece of clothing worn by men and women

yeast A substance made up of fungi that grow quickly

Index